W9-DIL-202

Avenue West
Falls, MN 36537
218...20...5586

WITHDRAWN

WHAT ARE THE SEVEN WONDERS OF THE WORLD?

WHAT ARE THE
7 NATURAL WONDERS
OF THE UNITED STATES?

Cheryl L. DeFries

Enslow Publishers, Inc.
40 Industrial Road
Box 398
Berkeley Heights, NJ 07922
USA

http://www.enslow.com

Copyright © 2013 by Enslow Publishers, Inc.

All rights reserved.

No part of this book may be reproduced by any means without the written permission of the publisher.

Original edition published as *Seven Natural Wonders of the United States and Canada* in 2005.

Library of Congress Cataloging-in-Publication Data

DeFries, Cheryl L.

    What are the 7 natural wonders of the United States? / Cheryl L. DeFries.

        p. cm.

    Summary: "Learn about the seven wonders of the United States: The Everglades, Glacier Point: Yosemite National Park, Grand Canyon, Mississippi River, Mount McKinley: Denali National Park, Niagara Falls and Redwood Forest"— Provided by publisher.

    Includes bibliographical references and index.

    ISBN 978-0-7660-4154-7

    1. National parks and reserves—United States—Juvenile literature. 2. Natural monuments—United States—Juvenile literature. I. Title. II. Title: What are the seven natural wonders of the United States?

    E160.D43 2013

    917.3—dc23

                                                            2012009143

Future editions:

Paperback ISBN: 978-1-4644-0233-3   EPUB ISBN: 978-1-4645-1152-3

Single-User PDF ISBN: 978-1-4646-1152-0   Multi-User PDF ISBN: 978-0-7660-5781-4

Printed in the United States of America

112012 Lake Book Manufacturing, Inc., Melrose Park, IL

10 9 8 7 6 5 4 3 2 1

To Our Readers: We have done our best to make sure all Internet addresses in this book were active and appropriate when we went to press. However, the author and the publisher have no control over and assume no liability for the material available on those Internet sites or on other Web sites they may link to. Any comments or suggestions can be sent by e-mail to comments@enslow.com or to the address on the back cover.

♻ Enslow Publishers, Inc., is committed to printing our books on recycled paper. The paper in every book contains 10% to 30% post-consumer waste (PCW). The cover board on the outside of each book contains 100% PCW. Our goal is to do our part to help young people and the environment too!

Photo Credits: © 2011 Photos.com, a division of Getty Images. All rights reserved., pp. 21, 37; ©Enslow Publishers, Inc., p.7; Adam Berent/© 2011 Photos.com, a division of Getty Images. All rights reserved., p. 35; Anton Foltin/© 2011 Photos.com, a division of Getty Images. All rights reserved., p. 18; Eric Foltz/© 2011 Photos.com, a division of Getty Images. All rights reserved., p. 22; Erik Meldrum/© 2011 Photos.com, a division of Getty Images. All rights reserved., p. 16; Jill Lang/© 2011 Photos.com, a division of Getty Images. All rights reserved., pp. 1, 4; Jiri Hera/© 2011 Photos.com, a division of Getty Images. All rights reserved., p. 12; Jupiterimages/© 2011 Photos.com, a division of Getty Images. All rights reserved., p. 10; pmphoto/© 2011 Photos.com, a division of Getty Images. All rights reserved., p. 40; rabbit75_ist/ © 2011 Photos.com, a division of Getty Images. All rights reserved., p. 8; Shutterstock.com, pp. 13, 32; Thinkstock/ © 2011 Photos.com, a division of Getty Images. All rights reserved., pp.26, 28, 30;

Cover Photo Credits: © 2011 Photos.com, a division of Getty Images. All rights reserved. (Grand Canyon); Jill Lang/ © 2011 Photos.com, a division of Getty Images. All rights reserved., (Niagara Falls); Shutterstock.com(The Everglades); Thinkstock/© 2011 Photos.com, a division of Getty Images. All rights reserved.(Mississippi River); Thinkstock/© 2011 Photos.com, a division of Getty Images. All rights reserved. (Mt. McKinley); pmphoto/© 2011 Photos.com, a division of Getty Images. All rights reserved.(Redwoods); Jill Lang/© 2011 Photos.com, a division of Getty Images. All rights reserved.,(Glacier Point)

Contents

Water cascades down American Falls. These are located on the New York Side of the falls.

SEVEN NATURAL WONDERS OF THE UNITED STATES

The Everglades

❈ Covers 1,296,500 acres (524,686 hectares)
❈ Everglades National Park in Florida is the largest designated wilderness area east of the Rocky Mountains
❈ Most significant breeding ground for tropical wading birds in North America

Glacier Point: Yosemite National Park

❈ Located in the California Sierra Nevada Mountains, 150 miles (241.4 kilometers) east of San Francisco
❈ Glacier Point is a 3,200-foot (975.4-meter) high granite cliff
❈ Yosemite Falls, which begins at Glacier Point, is the tallest waterfall in North America

Grand Canyon

❈ The Grand Canyon is about a mile (1.6 kilometers) deep from the top to its floor
❈ The Grand Canyon covers 1,217,403 acres (493,048 hectares)
❈ The black-bellied, white-tailed Kaibab squirrel lives on the North Rim of the Grand Canyon and its habitat has been named a National Natural Landmark

Mississippi River

❈ The Mississippi River is one of the world's busiest rivers
❈ At 2,350 miles (3,781 kilometers) long, it is the second longest river in North America
❈ Nearly a half million pounds (227,000 kilograms) of sediment are moved by the Mississippi River each day

Mount McKinley: Denali National Park

❈ At 20,320 feet (6,197.5 meters) high, Mount McKinley is the tallest mountain and highest point in North America
❈ Mount McKinley is part of the 600-mile (965.6 kilometer) long Alaska Mountain range
❈ The North Peak of Mount McKinley was first climbed by Peter Anderson and Bill Taylor on April 3, 1910

Niagara Falls

❈ Niagara Falls is located on the border of the United States and Canada
❈ Niagara Falls is the largest waterfall in North America and the second largest waterfall in the world
❈ The Niagara River's normal water flow is 212,000 cubic feet (6,003,170 liters) per second

Redwood Forest

❈ There are three types of redwood trees left in the world
❈ Giant sequoias can grow nearly 275 feet (83.8 meters) tall
❈ Coast redwoods average 350 feet (106.7 meters) in height and 18 feet (5.5 meters) in width

CHAPTER 1

Introducing the Wonders

Seven spectacular natural wonders can be enjoyed from coast to coast and border to border in the United States and Canada. Many of these marvels have been created over millions of years. Glaciers, water, ice, wind, erosion, and the movement of the earth's plates have produced them.

The location of these wonders varies quite a bit. On the East Coast is the Florida Everglades, a subtropical wetland. The subtropics are areas that border the tropical regions, and the Everglades is the largest subtropical wilderness in the United States. On the West Coast, California has two natural wonders. Glacier Point, in Yosemite National Park, is made of solid granite, and the tallest living trees in the world are found in the Redwood Forest. Alaska is home to Mount McKinley, the tallest mountain in North America. The Grand Canyon is in Arizona. The Canadian province of Ontario and the state of New York share the Niagara Falls, and the Mississippi River passes through ten states.

These seven natural wonders are all different, but they share something in common. They are majestic works of art, shaped by natural forces, seen and unseen by humans.

The United States and Canada are filled with natural wonders. We chose the seven that seemed to be the most famous and most studied. However,

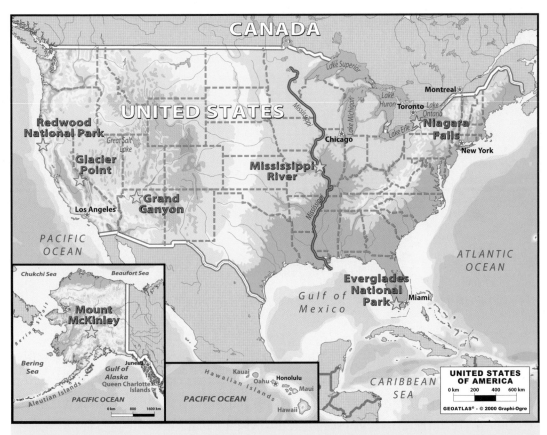

This map of the United States and part of Canada shows the location of each of the wonders profiled in this book.

there are many more. For example, two natural wonders can be found in Utah. The Rainbow Bridge is the world's largest natural bridge. Arches National Park has over one hundred natural sandstone arches.

Crater Lake, in southwest Oregon, is a blue lake in a volcanic crater. Death Valley in southwest Nevada and southeast California is a desert and the lowest point in the Western Hemisphere. Central Kentucky's Mammoth Cave is the longest cave system in the world.

A view of the Grand Canyon in the winter from the South Rim.

The Petrified Forest and part of the Painted Desert containing petrified trees and logs are in eastern Arizona. Yellowstone National Park is located in three states: Wyoming, Idaho, and Montana. Yellowstone is the home of hot springs, waterfalls, and a geyser called Old Faithful.

The four largest volcanoes on earth are located on the big island of Hawaii. They are Mauna Kea, Mauna Loa, Hualalai, and Kohala. Mauna Loa, in fact, is the largest active volcano in the world. California has the La Brea and McKittrick tar pits, which contain numerous preserved fossils.

Canada is home to the Bay of Fundy. This is the place that has the largest tides in the Atlantic Ocean.

As you can see, splendid natural wonders can be found throughout the United States and Canada. Nature has entrusted her treasures to the human race. It is our responsibility to protect and preserve these amazing creations for our generation and future generations.

CHAPTER 2

The Everglades

The eastern sky glowed a fiery orange as the sun rose and cast a warm glow on the bleached branches of a mangrove tree. A thin haze drifted close to the water, cloaking it in a veil of mystery. It was summertime in the Everglades, and the heat and humidity of midday had not yet moved the area's inhabitants into their usual drowsy but watchful state.

A young frog watched a droning dragonfly. It hopped from a lily pad onto the shore and watched the insect dart in and out among the reeds. The dragonfly skimmed the water and came to rest on the root of a cypress tree. The frog saw its chance for an early morning meal and sprang to life. It landed near a mud-covered, half-submerged log.

In a blink of an eye, the frog disappeared as the "log's" murderous jaws opened and shut.

As the mud settled back around the alligator, the air was filled with a machine-gun-like chatter. A dark form flew over the water. It was still dark enough that the bird was hidden from view; only the sound of its wings gave away its position. It braced its wings against the cool morning breeze and glided toward a sandbar. With a few sweeps of its large wings, it settled down, inches from its prey.

An aerial view of Everglades National Park in Florida

It plucked the apple snail from the ground, tossed it in the air, and with the skill of a juggler, hooked it on its beak. Two seconds later, the Everglades kite, an endangered bird, was airborne again. It flew to the limb of a tree just yards away where it safely removed the small animal from its shell.

This is life in the Florida Everglades. Wildlife kept alive by other wildlife, each dependent on a complex food chain that began thousands of years ago. Everglades National Park is home to more than seven hundred plants and three hundred birds. This is the only place in the world where both crocodiles and alligators live together. Fifteen endangered species make the Everglades their home. They include the American crocodile, the wood stork, the Atlantic Ridley turtle, and the Florida panther.[1]

Size and Location

Rainwater and excess water from Lake Okeechobee run southward, creating a one-of-a-kind wetlands area. Wetlands are areas that are usually marshlands or swamps where it is always moist, and many of the plant and animal species live in shallow pools of water. The Everglades covers a large area extending southwest from Lake Okeechobee to the Florida Bay and the Gulf of Mexico. This enormous marshland covers about five thousand square miles (thirteen thousand square kilometers), an area a little smaller than the state of Connecticut.

Establishment

In 1916, 4,000 acres (1,620 hectares) of marshland on Paradise Key became the first protected area in the Everglades. This marshland was called Royal Palm State Park. In 1934, President Franklin Delano Roosevelt signed an act to create a 2,164,480-acre (876,614-hectare) park to preserve the wilderness of the Everglades. After years of land purchases, 2,200 square miles (5,698 square kilometers) were set aside, and on December 6, 1947, President Harry S Truman dedicated Everglades National Park. This was the first national park established by the federal government in its effort to save and protect the environment and wildlife.

Additional efforts were made to preserve the Everglades. In 1968, Biscayne National Park was established, and 570,000 acres (230,850 hectares) of Big Cypress Swamp became a federal preserve in 1974. In 1973, the government had passed the Endangered Species Act. This national act protects particular species that are in danger of dying off, and it includes specific species in the Everglades.

Geology

South Florida appeared after the last Pleistocene Age, an era that occurred about ten thousand years ago. This low-lying wetland was created by the

Flocks of flamingos call Everglades National Park home.

overflow of water from melting glaciers. The highest point in the Everglades is only 8 feet (2.4 meters) above sea level.

Ecosystem

For years, hurricanes flooded southern Florida. To control the water and prevent flooding, a complex system of man-made canals, floodgates, dams, pump stations, and levees were built to control the floodwaters. These man-made structures, and land development, almost devastated the Everglades.

Destruction to the ecosystem (a community of living things and their environment) of the Everglades can happen when humans release water (from a structure such as a dam) and it is not properly timed with nature's

Fifteen endangered species make the Everglades their home, including this American crocodile.

natural cycles. The water can destroy alligator nests and feeding areas for all animals. The Everglades are left with too little water during times of drought. This occurs because water is drained off for human needs.

Water from agricultural runoff is the source of poisons to the Everglades' inhabitants. Mercury and other pollutants are now found in the area's wildlife, including animals and fish. Sea grass, which is essential to marine life, is also dying off in part because of pollution. Other problems in the Everglades are caused by drainage of wetlands, as well as hunting.

Recently, exotic, nonnative animals and plants have been appearing in the Everglades. These species include Burmese python snakes, iguanas,

Nile water monitors, and other predatory animals. Originally, they were introduced as pets, food sources, or for biological controls.[2] These species thrive in this climate. They are breeding, competing for food, and threatening the survival of local species. In addition, it is difficult to eliminate the exotic species without destroying the native animals and plants.

Some wildlife in the Everglades is now in danger of becoming extinct, meaning that there are no members of a species alive and the species is gone forever. Several species of reptiles, birds, and mammals, including the Garber's Spurge plant and Schaus Swallowtail butterfly, are on the U.S. Fish and Wildlife Service Endangered list.

About half of Florida's eighty-seven panthers live in the protected park of the Everglades. When the panthers' numbers dropped dramatically, eight female cougars were brought from Texas in 1995. Five of the female cougars bred with male panthers and produced healthy crossbred kittens.[3]

Conclusion

Land development has claimed a large part of the Everglades. Over half of the original Everglades no longer exists. Past efforts by the government have helped, but only one fifth of the original Everglades is protected.[4] Today, the Everglades National Park is one of the most endangered national parks in the United States.[5]

Recently, the state of Florida and the U.S. Congress approved $7.8 billion to fund a thirty-year Comprehensive Everglades Restoration Plan to rescue the Everglades. The plan is to increase and improve the storage, supply, and quality of water; slow the growth of nonnative plants; reestablish sheet flow (the flow of water across a surface); build a storm-water treatment center to filter and treat runoff water; and restore Lake Okeechobee.[6]

Clean water is the lifeblood of the Everglades.[7] The long-term goal is to provide a better quality of life for the wildlife and plants of the Everglades while addressing the growing needs of humans.

CHAPTER 3

Glacier Point: Yosemite National Park

The 761,266-acre (308,312-hectare) Yosemite National Park, about the size of the state of Rhode Island, is located in California's Sierra Nevada Mountains.[1] This park of gigantic granite rock formations is situated 150 miles (241.4 kilometers) east of San Francisco.

Location

Glacier Point is located at the tip of a very steep 3,200-foot (975.4-meter) high granite cliff. Views from this vantage point provide an amazing wide-open vista of Yosemite Valley. The Sierra Nevada Mountains are visible, as is the Merced River below Glacier Point.

Fast-moving water and glaciers carved the canyon of Yosemite Valley and created elevations ranging from 2,000 to 13,000 feet (609.6 to 3,965 meters) above sea level. The different elevations supply a wide variety of landscapes to visitors of Yosemite National Park. Some of the park's superb scenery includes rumbling waterfalls, magnificent granite cliffs, giant sequoia groves, and massive rock formations.

History

Millions of years ago, sediment on the seabed combined with the earth's movements to begin creation of the Sierra Nevada Mountain Range. About

Glacier Point is located in Yosemite National Park. It is part of the Sierra Nevada Mountain Range.

10 million years ago, the sediment rose above sea level as the earth shifted. At the same time, granite was formed when hot liquefied rock rose up from the earth's core and cooled under the sediment. Over time, weather conditions wore away the sediment, exposing the granite of the Sierra Nevada Mountain Range.[2]

Rapid water flow from the Merced River created the V-shaped Yosemite Valley. When the Ice Age produced glaciers, these gigantic masses of ice widened and deepened the canyon, carving it into a U-shaped valley. Water found its way over some of the hanging valleys and became magnificent waterfalls.[3]

From Glacier Point, Yosemite Falls provides a spectacular display. There are actually three separate falls. The Upper Yosemite Falls drops 1,430 feet (436.1 meters); the Middle Cascades Falls drops 675 feet (205.7 meters); and the Lower Yosemite Falls drops 320 feet (97.5 meters). Combining the free-falling water from the three falls makes it the tallest waterfall in North America.

The view from Glacier Point also reveals the colossal Half Dome, an imposing granite monument that rises 4,000 feet (1,220 meters) above the valley floor. Another splendid rock structure is El Capitan, which rises vertically almost 3,000 feet (915 meters) above the canyon.

Falling rocks are a common occurrence in the park. Several natural events contribute to rockfalls. When water gets into rock crevices, a series of freezes and thaws can cause the rock to split. Temperature changes, combined with the movements in the earth's crust, also weaken the rocks.[4]

In recent years, Glacier Point was the site of two major rockfalls. In 1996, an 80,000-ton (72,624-metric ton) boulder of granite broke loose. It slid 500 feet (152.4 meters) before free-falling 400 feet (121.9 meters). Then in 1999, a 525-ton (476.6-metric ton) boulder broke loose.

The view from Glacier Point reveals the colossal Half Dome, an imposing granite monument that rises 4,000 feet above the valley floor.

Plant and Animal Life

The park is home to black bears, California bighorn sheep, golden eagles, coyotes, and mule deer. Also found in the park are the endangered or threatened great gray owl and peregrine falcon.

Twenty-seven varieties of trees are in the park, and four are easy to identify due to their massive size. They are the giant sequoia tree, California black oak, incense cedar, and the ponderosa pine.[5]

There are an estimated 10,500 bighorn sheep left in the wild in California.

Threats

Concerns affecting the park include fire, air quality, and the high volume of visitors. Also, the introduction of nonnative plant and animal species have threatened the native wildlife and vegetation. Glacier Point received $3.2 million of public and private funds for restoration in September 1997. These funds paid for things such as improvements to trails, park facilities, wildlife management, and more. Although the National Park Service oversaw the restoration, no federal dollars were used.[6]

Grand Canyon

The Grand Canyon is known around the world for its astonishing vastness and the multicolored rocks that line the canyon walls. The colors in the rocks come from different minerals. A perfectly preserved history record is found in the magnificently stacked layers of rock. As each layer is revealed, it tells a tale from a different era.

Location and Size

The Grand Canyon is located in the northwestern section of the state of Arizona. Beginning at Lees Ferry, Arizona, the canyon runs 217 miles (349.2 kilometers) and ends at Grand Wash Cliffs, Arizona. The canyon is about a mile deep from the top to its floor and covers 1,217,403 acres (493,048 hectares), or an area about the size of the state of Delaware.

Description

There are three different areas in the Grand Canyon National Park: the South Rim, the North Rim, and Inner Canyon or Inner Gorge. The width between the South and North rims is about one-half mile (one kilometer) in some areas and as wide as 18 miles (29 kilometers) in other areas.

This image of the Grand Canyon shows its astonishing vastness and the multicolored rocks that line the canyon walls.

On the South Rim, the elevation is 7,000 feet (2,135 meters). The North Rim is higher; the elevations range from 7,870 to 8,825 feet (2,400.3 to 2,691.6 meters). Weather conditions and temperatures are different in the each section of the park. The South Rim receives about 16 inches (40.6 centimeters) of yearly rainfall while the North Rim receives about 26 inches stack (66 centimeters) of rain annually. Summertime temperatures vary from 50°F to 80°F (10°C to 26.7°C) on the South Rim while the North Rim is 5° to 10° cooler. Winter weather conditions on the South Rim can bring a combination of heavy snow, fog, and ice. The South Rim has more visitors because it is easier to reach and it is open all year. Winter on the North Rim can cause very hazardous conditions. This rim is closed to visitors from October until May.

Over the course of 6 million years, the Colorado River eroded the earth to form the Grand Canyon.

Over time, the force of the Colorado River ate through the surface of the Colorado Plateau. As the layers of the plateau were exposed, the canyon walls uncovered a variety of colorful rock layers. Each layer contains deposits of minerals and sediment that are different from the layers above and below it. All layers reveal a different history from its era.

The oldest rock layers, called Brahma and Vishnu Schist, are closest to the bottom of the canyon. This rock is approximately 2 billion years old. On top of these layers is the 1.7-billion-year-old Zoroaster granite rock. Additional rock layers range from 1.2 billion years old to the top layer (Kaibab limestone), which is approximately 250 million years old. In the upper rock layers there is evidence of rich marine life, but older rocks like the Vishnu Schist layer yield no record of life.[1]

Due to the fact that the North Rim slopes southward, rain and snow runoff spills down into the canyon, causing erosion to this wall. Erosion from runoff is less on the South Rim as the water flows away from the rim.[2]

Animal and Plant Life

Animals found on the South Rim include the bobcat, gray fox, bighorn sheep, mountain lion, mule deer, coyotes, and rock squirrels. The Albert squirrel only lives on this side of the canyon. Some trees found on this rim are the pinyon pine and Utah juniper.

The black-bellied, white-tailed Kaibab squirrel lives on the North Rim and is only found on the Kaibab Plateau in northern Arizona. Because it is considered a unique habitat, it has the special designation of a National Natural Landmark it habitat, not the species, has been designated a National Natural Landmark.[3] Mountain lions, northern goshawks, bobcats, and the ponderosa pine tree are found on the North Rim. Only on the North Rim can you find blue spruce and fir trees.

Several types of nonpoisonous snakes and four different types of rattlesnakes, including the Grand Canyon rattlesnake, live in the Inner Canyon.

Jaguars, grizzly bears, wolves, and river otters are a few examples of species that no longer exist within the Grand Canyon because of humans.[4] Man-made dams have changed food sources and nesting areas. Nonnative species, such as trout, have been introduced and are eating native species like the endangered humpback chub fish. Human trash and other items are eaten by animals and fish, causing death or serious injury.

According to the National Park Service, twenty-three animals and plants listed on the Threatened and Endangered Species List live in the park or in the area near the park.[5] Continuing environmental problems being addressed by the National Park Service are fire, air quality that is affected by industrial pollution outside the park, water quality, and tourism.

CHAPTER 5

Mississippi River

The Mississippi River has a major impact on the economy and ecology in North America. Commercially, it is one of the world's busiest rivers. In 1988, Congress created the Mississippi National River and Recreation Area to protect this national treasure.

Location

At about 2,350 miles (3,781 kilometers) the Mississippi River is the second longest river in North America. Its drainage basin (the area from which all the water in the river and streams drains) covers 1,837,000 square miles (4,757,830 square kilometers). All or part of the land of thirty-one states and two Canadian provinces drain into the river.[1]

A branch of the Mississippi River, the 2,540-mile (4,087-kilometer) long Missouri River, is North America's longest river. Together, the merging waters of the Mississippi-Missouri rivers make it the fourth longest river on the globe.

Three different regions make up the Mississippi River. The beginning water source for the Mississippi is called "the headwaters." The headwaters include the water from Lake Itasca, located in the Minnesota North Woods, down to St. Anthony Falls in Minneapolis, Minnesota.

A second region, called the Upper Mississippi River, starts at St. Anthony Falls. It flows downstream to Cairo, Illinois. The mouth of the Ohio River is in this area.

The third region is the Lower Mississippi River. It runs southward from Cairo to Head of Passes in the Gulf of Mexico.

The Mississippi River has the third largest drainage basin in the world, exceeded only by the drainage basin of the Amazon and Congo rivers.[2] Each day, an average of 436,000 tons of sediment (soil and other organic matter) are moved by the Mississippi River. Sediment, also called alluvium, is deposited along the delta. Over time, these daily deposits form new land.

Commerce on the Mississippi

Commercial ships on the river carry 92 percent of the United States' agricultural exports, 78 percent of the world's exports in feed grains and soybeans, and most of the livestock and hogs produced nationally.[3]

People living in towns, farms, cities, and villages along the Mississippi River depend on the water for drinking, growing crops, raising animals, making food, and recreation. Industry relies on the freshwater to produce energy.

Geology

The Mississippi River's natural landscape is varied. Beginning with an elevation of 1,475 feet (449.6 meters) above sea-level, the face of the river changes many times on its way to the sea-level delta. There are magnificent white sandstone cliffs, a gorge, a waterfall, valleys, swamps, bayous, and floodplains (flat areas along the river that flood naturally).

Flooding is frequent along the river. When snow and ice from northern and western winters melt and the ground is frozen, the soil is unable to absorb the extra water. The excess water overflows the banks of the rivers and streams, causing flooding.

An aerial view of the Mississippi River as it flows through Iowa

While flooding sometimes threatens communities and industry, it is needed to wash away the buildup of debris. This action clears and cleans the area for agriculture and animal and bird nests, as well as increasing the food supply for fish, fowl, and people.

Plant and Animal Life

The largest connecting wetland structure in North America is found along the Mississippi River. The river and its floodplains are the habitats of a variety of living species.

Forty percent of the nation's migratory waterfowl and 60 percent of all North American birds—a total of 326 species—use the river and its basin during migration. One hundred forty-five different amphibians and reptiles inhabit the Upper Mississippi River.

Twenty-five percent of all North American fish swim in the waters of the Mississippi River. The upper part of the river is home to thirty-eight different species of mussels while the lower part of the Mississippi may have as many as sixty different species of mussels.[4] The salty waters in the lower delta produce enormous quantities of shrimp and fish.

Important crops from the Mississippi region include rice, cotton, and sugarcane. The delta yields sulfur, oil, and natural gas.[5]

Threats

Humans have significantly changed the natural flow of the river. The changes were made to accommodate commercial shipping and development. Locks, dams, and levees have been built. The Environmental Protection Agency says that fifty cities depend on the Mississippi River for their daily water supply.[6]

People are responsible for polluting the Mississippi River by using pesticides on farms and chemicals in industry that seep into the river. This causes environmental destruction, which directly affects the plants, animals, and marine life that make the river and the watershed their home.

An aerial view of the swamplands on the Mississippi River, New Orleans, Louisiana

Conclusion

Steps to protect the Mississippi River and other waterways are necessary. The Mississippi River and Tributaries Project has addressed four major elements. They are levees for flood control, floodways for excess water flow, channel improvement to help navigation, and tributary basin improvements for major drainage and flood control.[7]

CHAPTER 6

Mount McKinley: Denali National Park

Clouds often hide Alaska's Mount McKinley, the tallest mountain and highest point in North America. It is one of the world's Seven Summits, a group consisting of only the tallest mountains on each of the world's seven continents. The massive snow- and ice-covered Mount McKinley reaches a staggering 20,320 feet (6,197.6 meters) into the sky. Most other mountains in this range are between 7,000 to 9,000 feet (2,135 to 2,745 meters) high.

The sheer size of this mountain dominates the skyline. It can been seen from 200 miles (321.9 kilometers) away on Cook's Inlet and observed from Fairbanks, which lies 150 miles (241.4 kilometers) north of Mount McKinley. The mammoth height of the mountain, combined with below-zero temperatures on the summit and fierce wind gusts, makes Mount McKinley one of the coldest places in the world.

Location

McKinley is located in the Denali National Park and Preserve in the south central region of Alaska. Denali National Park and Preserve covers 6,075,000 acres (2,460,375 hectares) or over 9,400 square miles (24,345.9 square kilometers). This is just slightly smaller than the size of the state of Massachusetts.[1] Denali is located 130 miles (209.2 kilometers) north-northwest of Anchorage, Alaska, and the closest town is Talkeetna, located 55 miles (88.5 kilometers) southeast.

Mount McKinley in Denali National Park in Alaska

Naming a Mountain

Ancient Athabaskan Indians called the mountain now known as Mount McKinley "Denali," which means "The Great One" or "The High One." Later in history, people in different parts of the state called it by different names: Doleyka, Traleika, Bulshia, Gora, and Tenada.[2]

In 1889, the mountain was named Densmore's Peak after prospector Frank Densmore. However this was changed in 1896. A prospector named W. A. Dickey named the mountain Mount McKinley after a senator who later became the twenty-fifth president of the United States, William McKinley.

Geology

Millions of years ago, movements by the Pacific crustal plate (the outer layer of the earth) and the North Atlantic plate created mountains. One of the mountain ranges that was formed was the Alaska Range. McKinley is part of the 600-mile (965.6-kilometer) long Alaska Mountain Range.

Mount McKinley has two peaks: the South Peak (20,320 feet or 6,197.6 meters high) and the North Peak (19,470 feet or 5,938.3 meters high). Snow-fields cover over 50 percent of McKinley. The mountain's core is made of slate and granite and is covered by ice that is hundreds of feet thick in some places.[3]

The steep southern slope of the mountain extends out for 12 miles (19.3 kilometers) and is 17,000 feet (5,185 meters) high. Five major ridges extend from the summit and many spurs jut out from the ridges.[4]

About 17 percent of Denali National Park's land area is covered with glaciers. On the south side of the Alaskan Range are five large glaciers: Kahiltna, Ruth, Eldridge, Tokositna, and Yentna. On Mount McKinley and on the north side of the mountain range is the largest glacier, Muldrow Glacier, which is 34 miles (54.7 kilometers) long.

Hundreds of small earthquakes occur in the park each year. Most earthquakes happen beneath Mount McKinley and measure an average of 2.2 magnitude on the Richter Scale.

A mountaineering team ascends the upper Kahiltna Glacier to their camp at 11,200 feet, at around midnight, on Denali, Denali National Park, Alaska.

Climbing History

On April 3, 1910, a mountain-climbing party made up of Peter Anderson and Bill Taylor successfully climbed the North Peak of Mount McKinley. Another team made up of Harry Karstens, Reverend Hudson Stuck, Walter Harper, and Robert Tatum, was successful in conquering the South Peak of Mount McKinley on June 7, 1913.[5] Barbara Polk Washburn was the first woman to reach the summit, on June 6, 1947.

Denali National Park and Preserve

Charles Sheldon, a naturalist and game hunter, became concerned about the decline in the mountain's wildlife, especially the Dall bighorn sheep. Wildlife numbers were dwindling because gold prospectors and construction crews hunted game for food.[6] Sheldon is credited with leading the way to establish this vast wilderness as a National Park. On February 26, 1917, his efforts were rewarded when McKinley National Park was created as a game refuge. The park combined with Denali National Monument (1978) and became known as the Denali National Park and Preserve in 1980.

Wildlife

According to the National Park Service, Denali National Park is home to thirty-nine species of mammals. Some larger animals are the Dall bighorn sheep, brown bears, grizzly bears, wolves, moose, and caribou. Some smaller mammals can also survive in this harsh winter climate. Ground squirrels and marmots hibernate in the winter. Meanwhile, red squirrels and beavers live on food they have stored up for the winter. Weasels and snowshoe hares live outside during the winter, but they have developed a way to hide from predators. Their fur turns white to blend with the snow.

There are 167 species of birds living in the park, including the once-endangered peregrine falcon. Three different species of salmon, seven different types of fish in all, and one amphibian, called the wood frog, also live in the park.

Conclusion

Fire, caused by lightning, is the biggest natural threat to Denali. The park offers a fantastic opportunity to study the climate, glaciers, fire, and human-induced changes such as pollution of the air and water. Park employees constantly monitor the environment to help protect the natural resources.[7]

CHAPTER 7

Niagara Falls

Niagara Falls is on the Niagara River and shares the border between the United States and Canada. It is located halfway between Lake Erie and Lake Ontario.

Two Sides to the Story

Niagara Falls consists of three separate waterfalls. The two falls of the United States are called the American Falls and the Bridal Veil Falls. The Bridal Veil Falls sits directly south of the American Falls and is sometimes called the Iris Falls. They are located on the western side of New York State in the city of Niagara Falls. The third fall, the Canadian Horseshoe Falls, is in the Canadian city of Niagara Falls, across the border in southeastern Ontario, Canada.

History

Niagara Falls, which is made of dolostone limestone (limestone that includes a lot of the mineral dolomite), shale, and sandstone, is the largest waterfall in North America and the second largest in the world. Only the 5,500-foot (1,676.4-meter) Victoria Falls, on the Zambezi River in southern Africa, is larger.

he American Falls is also called the Rainbow Falls. This is because rainbows are rmed when the morning sun shines through the mist of the falling water.

Niagara Falls exists because of the 2-billion-year-old Niagara Escarpment, a long cliff created by erosion. The escarpment extends from eastern Wisconsin through Niagara Falls, and ends in Rochester, New York. When the glaciers of the Ice Age receded, Lake Erie overflowed, and erosion caused by ice and water gave birth to the Niagara River. In turn, the twelve-thousand-year-old river carved out gorges. These gorges became the Niagara Falls.

Three times in recorded history, the thundering roar of water over the falls became silent. In 1848, ice jammed the Niagara River preventing the water from reaching the falls. Dam-building along the River, stopped the flow to the Canadian Horseshoe Falls in 1953. The American Falls were drained in 1969 to see whether rocks could be removed to give the falls a more attractive appearance. The project was canceled because it was too costly.

Size

Canada's Horseshoe Falls is wider than the American Falls, but the water flowing over the American Falls drops farther than the Canadian Falls. Horseshoe Falls is 2,200 feet (670.6 meters) wide. The water falls nearly 173 feet (52.7 meters) into the Maid of the Mist Pool. When the water in the Niagara River reaches the Horseshoe Falls, it is traveling about twenty miles per hour (thirty-two kilometers per hour). Ninety percent of the water from the Niagara River flows over the Horseshoe Falls.

Combined, the American Falls and the Bridal Veil Falls are 1,156 feet (352.3 meters) wide. Luna Island is a thin piece of land that separates the two American falls. Water plunges down 176 feet (53.6 meters) to the bottom of the American Falls but due to broken rock, known as talus, that has built up at the bottom of the falls, the water actually falls 70 feet (21.3 meters).[1] Because Goat Island is in front of the American and Bridal Veil falls, water is rerouted. Only 10 percent of the Niagara River water flow reaches the American Falls.

The American Falls is also called the Rainbow Falls. This is because rainbows are formed when the morning sun shines through the mist of the falling water.

Water from the Niagara River, which flows over the falls, drains an area of 264,000 miles (424,776 kilometers), including water from Lake Erie, Lake Michigan, Lake Huron, and Lake Superior.[2] As the water flows away from the falls to the Atlantic Ocean, it passes through Lake Ontario and then becomes part of the St. Lawrence River.

Natural Phenomenon

As the water rushes over the falls, some of the mist evaporates. This process forms a chemical called calcium carbonate. This chemical mixes with algae in the water.[3] The algae contain a chemical called chlorophyll. When the two chemicals combine, they create foam. As the foam combines with water and floats away from the falls, it dissolves in the water.

Canada's Horseshoe Falls is wider than the American Falls.

A magnificent whirlpool is found in the area of the waterfalls. A whirlpool is formed when opposite water currents meet, creating a circular downward spiral motion of water.

The Horseshoe Falls has never frozen, but the American Falls has frozen six times because less water flows over it.[4] Winter can bring ice formations when water and mist from the falls mix and freeze. The ice will begin to appear on the banks of the river and the banks of the Horseshoe Falls. During very cold winters, ice formations can stretch across the entire river, creating an ice bridge.

Reservoirs

The Niagara Falls area is the site of the world's first hydroelectric power station. Canada's power station, the Sir Adam Beck No. 2 Generating Station, was built in 1954, and the Robert Moses Niagara Power Plant on the American side was built in 1961.[5] Seventy percent of Canada's electricity comes from hydropower, and most of it comes from the Sir Adam Beck generators.

Both Canada's Ontario Hydro and the United States' New York State Power Authority own and operate the hydroelectric dam. Since the slant in the riverbed directs water toward the Canadian side, the dam is located there.

Normally, the Niagara River's water flow is 212,000 cubic feet (6,003,170 liters) per second.[6] Both governments agreed to maintain the water flow over the falls at 100,000 cubic feet (2,831,680 liters) per second from April 1 until October 31 so that tourists can see this enormous amount of water as it provides a spectacular display. In the evening and in winter, the water flow is restricted to 50,000 cubic feet (1,415,840 liters) per second. The diverted water travels underground to fill up the Ontario reservoir and the American Robert Moses Hydro reservoir.

Conclusion

Over years, the roaring water has eaten away at the bedrock and moved the escarpment (the slope of the falls) back 7 miles (11.3 kilometers) upriver from its original location.[7] However since dams were built and the hydroelectric plant has been in operation, erosion has slowed down in the falls area.

CHAPTER 8

Redwood Forest

A million years ago, dozens of species of the redwood grew in Asia, Europe, and western North America. Global climate changes caused all but three of the redwood species to disappear.

Types of Redwoods

In North America, two species survived. One is the coast redwood (*Sequoia sempervirens*), which lives along the Pacific Coast. It is the only place in the world where coast redwoods grow in their natural state. This 450-mile (724.1-kilometer) stretch of coast redwoods extends from Monterey County in northern California into a small portion of southwestern Oregon.

The second species found in North America is the giant sequoia (*Sequoiadendron giganteum*). They are found between elevations of 5,000 and 7,000 feet (1,524 and 2,133.6 meters) in the California Sierra Nevada Mountains. These massive trees live in scattered groves on the moist western side of the mountain slopes.

An isolated area in central China is home to the third type of redwood species, the dawn redwood (*Metasequoia glyptostroboides*). It is also known as the water larch.

The redwood trees located along the coast of California are the tallest trees in the world.

Size and Age

The tallest trees in the world are the coast redwoods. These trees average 350 feet (106.7 meters) in height and 18 feet (5.5 meters) in width. Over a dozen trees exceeding 360 feet (109.7 meters) in height are now growing along the California coast.[1]

The tallest documented living tree in the world is a coast redwood nicknamed the Mendocino Tree. It is about eight hundred years old, and stands 367.5 feet (112 meters) tall. The Mendocino Tree is located in the Montgomery Woods State Reserve, west of Ukiah, California.

The giant sequoias can reach heights of nearly 275 feet (83.8 meters). The tallest documented giant sequoia tree is named General Sherman, after the Civil War hero. This tree is located in the center of the Giant Forest, which is part of the Sequoia National Park. General Sherman is 274.9 feet (83.8 meters) high, and the trunk's circumference is 102.6 feet (31.3 meters). Another giant called General Grant is 268.1 feet (81.7 meters). It is just about 7 feet shorter than General Sherman, but General Grant's trunk is thicker, measuring 107.5 feet (32.8 meters) around.[2]

It takes between four hundred and five hundred years for redwoods to mature. The oldest living giant sequoia is located in Yosemite National Park. The tree is named the Grizzly Giant and is over 2,700 years old.

Climate

Redwoods in North America flourish on the northern Pacific Coast where temperatures are moderate, moisture is plentiful, and the soil is well drained. They would be unable to grow in areas where winters are too harsh and summers too hot, or where there is not enough rain.

Physical Characteristics

The root system of the redwood is very shallow. Although the roots spread out in a 50-foot (15.2-meter) diameter, they only reach 6 to 10 feet (1.8 to 3 meters) into the earth.[3]

The redwood's reddish-brown bark is protected from fire, insects, and disease by a bitter chemical called tannic acid. Unlike many types of trees, flammable pitch and sap are not found in its bark.

As the tree ages, branches fall off the lower half of the trunk. If a tree is cut, damaged, burned, or affected by flooding, it has a way to renew itself. At the base of the tree is a dormant bulge called a burl or lignotuber. New stems are sent out from the burl. This results in what is known as a "fairy ring" or circle of new trees.[4] The ability to regenerate helps the redwood avoid extinction.

Growth

Young redwood saplings can grow up to 6 feet (1.8 meters) a year. Coast redwood and giant sequoias are conifers, meaning they do not lose their leaves and they produce cones.

The redwoods take five to fifteen years to produce their first seeds from the cones. Each year, seeds are released, but only one in a million will grow into a redwood.

Forest Ecology

Redwoods require high moisture levels and take in between 35 and 100 inches (88.9 and 254 centimeters) of rain annually.[5] Redwoods receive most of their moisture from the winter rains and foggy summers.

When fog condenses (changes to liquid) on the leaves at the top of the tree, raindrops fall. Redwoods depend on the fog for additional water.

Living redwood branches provide homes for small animals and birds. The decaying leaves of the trees provide food for fungi and snails. Fallen branches or stumps become homes to animals, insects, and plants.

Threats

Humans are the number-one threat to redwoods. Logging had depleted 95 percent of the original redwood forest before redwoods became protected in the late 1960s. The industry still threatens redwoods in areas where the trees are growing for a second time. In addition, land development has damaged root systems, making trees unstable.

The biggest natural threat to a redwood is the wind. A damaged root system can cause a redwood to topple when wind combines with heavy rain or flooding.

Humans realized that the redwoods would disappear without intervention. In 1968, the Redwood National Park was established. It is a slender band of land 46 miles (74 kilometers) long and 11 miles (17.7 kilometers) wide. Now, future generations will enjoy these majestic trees.

Glossary

delta—Fan-shaped stretch of land formed at the lower end of a river by a buildup of sediments carried downstream and dropped off when currents or tides can no longer carry them.

drainage basin—The entire area that drains into a river or the tributaries of that river.

ecosystem—System of interactions between a community of living organisms and their environment.

erosion—To wear away, loosen, or dissolve land or soil by glacial ice, water, or wind.

extinct—When no more of a species exists on earth.

geology—The scientific study of the origin, history, and structure of the earth based on information collected from its rocks.

glacier—Large and slow-moving mass of ice.

gorge—Deep, narrow canyon or part of a canyon.

prospector—A person who inspects an area to see if there are any deposits of minerals.

reservoir—Place where water is collected and stored.

snowfield—Stretch of permanent snow located at the head of a glacier.

subtropical—Pertaining to the areas that border the tropics. The tropics are the areas between the Tropic of Cancer and the Tropic of Capricorn.

watershed—A land area that drains into a specific body of water.

wetland—Area that is wet or flooded on a regular basis.

Chapter Notes

Chapter 2. The Everglades

1. National Geographic Staff, *Guide To The National Parks: East and Midwest* (Washington, D.C.: National Geographic Society, 2001), p. 41.

2. South Florida National Park, *Park Guide: Surviving a Quiet Disaster* (Washington, D.C.: The National Park Foundation, December 2003), p.14.

3. Ibid.

4. U.S. Army Corps of Engineers Jacksonville District, *The Journey to Restore America's Everglades* (Jacksonville, Fla.: Department of the Army, 1999), p. 3.

5. Deborah Nordeen, "South Florida's Watery Wilderness Park Nears 50," *Everglades National Park,* January 6, 1999, <http://www.nps.gov/ever/eco/nordeen.htm> (February 17, 2004).

6. U.S. Army Corps of Engineers Jacksonville District, p. 5.

7. Doreen Russo, *AAA Guide to the National Parks* (New York: Collier Books, 1994), p. 78.

Chapter 3. Glacier Point: Yosemite Park

1. National Park Service, "Facts," Yosemite National Park, n.d., <http://www.nps.gov/yose/pphtml/facts.html> (March 24, 2004).

2. *Yosemite News,* "Yosemite Natural History," p. 1, 1962, 2004, <http://www .yosemitenews .com/natural_history.html> (March 12, 2004).

3. APN Media, "Yosemite: History," *American Park Network,* p. 3, 2001, <http://www. americanparknetwork.com/parkinfo/content.asp?catid=85&contenttypeid=10>(March 31, 2004).

4. Yosemite Association, "Frequently Asked Questions About Yosemite," *Visitor Information,* n.d., <http://www.yosemite.org/visitor/frequent-geology.htm> (March 24, 2004).

5. National Park Service, "Yosemite National Park," *US National Parks Net,* 2002, <http://www .yosemite.national-park.com/info.htm> (November 21, 2003).

6. APN Media, "Glacier Point: A Better View," *American Park Network,* <http://www .americanparknetwork.com/parkinfo/yo/aag/view.html> (March 31, 2004).

Chapter 4. Grand Canyon

1. Seymour L. Fishbein, *Grand Canyon Country/Its Majesty and Its Lore* (Washington, D.C.: National Geographic Society, 1991), p. 85.

2. Ibid., p. 38.

3. National Park Service, "Life in the Canyon," *Views of the National Park,* n.d., <http://www2 .nature.nps.gov/synthesis/views/Sites/GRCA/HTML/ET_01_Life.htm> (March 29, 2004).

4. Ibid., p. 5.

5. National Park Service, "Threatened and Endangered Species in the Grand Canyon Area," July 19, 2003, *Grand Canyon National Park,* <http://nps.gov/grca/resources/te.htm> (March 29, 2004).

Chapter 5. Mississippi River

1. U.S. Army Corps of Engineers, "The Mississippi River," *The Mississippi River and Tributaries Project,* May 19, 2004, <http://www.mvn.usace.army.mil/pao/bro/misstrib .htm> (September 9, 2004).

2. Ibid.

3. National Park Service, "General Information About the Mississippi River," *Mississippi National River and Recreation Area,* April 12, 2004, <http://www.nps.gov/miss/features/factoids/index.html> (September 9, 2004).

4. Ibid.

5. Columbia University Press, "Mississippi," *HistoryChannel.com,* 2003, <http://www .historychannel.com.perl/print_book.pl?ID=101590> (September 9, 2004).

6. National Park Service, "General Information About the Mississippi River."

7. U.S. Army Corps of Engineers, "The Mississippi River."

Chapter 6. Mount McKinley: Denali National Park

1. Alaskan.com, "Denali National Park," 2000, <www.alaskan.com/docs/denali1.html> (March 26, 2004).

2. Denali Summer Times, "Mount McKinley," March 10, 2004, <http://www .denalisummertimes .com/pages/McKinley.html> (September 9, 2004).

3. Alaskan.com, "Denali National Park."

4. Peakware, "Mount McKinley," *Peakware World Mountain Encyclopedia,* 2002, <http:// peakware.com/encyclopedia/peaks/mckinley.htm> (September 9, 2004).

5. Harry Kikstra, "Denali: Summit of North America," *The 7 Summits,* 2004, <http://7summits .com/denali/denali.php> (September 9, 2004).

6. National Park Service, "Denali National Park and Preserve," *Prehistory of Alaska,* n.d., <http:// www.nps.gov/akso/akarc/cr_dena.htm> (September 9, 2004).

7. National Park Service, "Nature & Science: Environmental Factors," *Denali National Park and Preserve,* n.d., <http://www.nps.gov/dena/pphtml/environmentalfactors.html> (September 9, 2004).

Chapter 7. Niagara Falls

1. Niagara Falls Live.com, "Facts About Niagara Falls," n.d., <http://www.niagarafallslive.com/ Facts_about_Niagara_Falls.htm> (September 9, 2004).

2. Info Niagara, "The Niagara River: A National Wonder," 2004, <http://www.infoniagara.com/ d-att-river.html> (September 9, 2004).

3. "Thunder Alley," Niagara Falls Frequently Asked Questions, n.d., <http://www.iaw .com/~falls/faq.html> (March 18, 2004).

4. "Does the Falls freeze in Winter?" *Niagara Falls Frequently Asked Questions,* n.d., <http://www .iaw.com/~falls/faq.html> (March 18, 2004).

5. Info Niagara, "The Niagara River: A National Wonder."

6. *Niagara Falls Frequently Asked Questions,* n.d., <http://www.iaw.com/~falls/ faq.html> (March 18, 2004).

7. Reader's Digest Editors, *Natural Wonders* (Pleasantville, N.Y.: Reader's Digest Association, Inc., 1997), p. 25.

Chapter 8. Redwood Forest

1. Sempervirens Fund, "The Coast Redwoods: The World's Tallest Trees," *Amazing Redwood Trees,* n.d., <http://www.sempervirens.org/sequoiasemp.htm> (February 18, 2004).

2. Wendell D. Flint, "The Giant Sequoia—Forest Masterpiece," *National Park Service,* 2002, <http://www.nps.gov/seki/bigtrees.htm> (September 9, 2004).

3. Ladywildlife, "The Redwood Forest and its Wildlife," 1996–2002, <http://ladywildlife.com/ animal/theredwoodforestanditswildlife.html> (September 9, 2004).

4. Chris Brinegar, Ph.D, "Ask the Redwood Doctor," *Amazing Redwood Trees,* Fall 2003, <http:www.sempervirens.org/doctor.htm> (September 9, 2004).

5. Barbara Holzman, "Redwood Forest," *Point Reyes Ecosystem Field Trip,* n.d., <http://www.sfsu .edu/~geog/bholzman/ptreyes/tripredf.htm> (November 21, 2003).

Further Reading and Internet Addresses

Further Reading

Augustin, Byron and Jake Kubena. *The Grand Canyon.* New York: Marshall Cavendish Benchmark, 2010.

Hurley, Michael. *The World's Most Amazing Mountains.* Chicago: Raintree, 2009.

Lynch, Wayne. *The Everglades.* Minnetonka, Minn.: NorthWord Books for Young Readers, 2007.

Roop, Peter and Connie Roop. *River Roads West: America's First Highways.* Honesdale, Pa.: Calkins Creek, 2007.

Woods, Michael and Mary B. Woods. *Seven Natural Wonders of North America.* Minneapolis, Minn.: Twenty-First Century Books, 2009.

Internet Addresses

Brainteaser: Grand Canyon—National Geographic Kids
<http://kids.nationalgeographic.com/staticfiles/NGS/NGKids/Game/GameFiles/brainteaser/grandcanyon/games_grandcanyon_brain.swf?rand=50000z>

Where to see Mt. McKinley-Denali 101
<www.denali101.com/denalinationalpark/see_mt_Mckinley.html>

Index